Richard Temple

An Application of Some General Political Rules

To the Present State of Great-Britain, Ireland and America - In a letter to

the Right Honourable Earl Temple

Richard Temple

An Application of Some General Political Rules
*To the Present State of Great-Britain, Ireland and America - In a letter to the Right
Honourable Earl Temple*

ISBN/EAN: 9783337195755

Printed in Europe, USA, Canada, Australia, Japan

Cover: Foto ©Suzi / pixelio.de

More available books at **www.hansebooks.com**

❀❀❀❀❀❀❀❀❀❀❀❀❀❀:❀❀:❀❀❀❀❀❀❀❀❀❀❀

A N

APPLICATION

O F

POLITICAL RULES,

T O

GREAT-BRITAIN,

IRELAND AND AMERICA.

❀❀❀❀❀❀❀:❀❀❀❀❀❀❀❀❀❀❀:❀❀❀❀❀❀

[Price One Shilling and Six-pence.]

A N

APPLICATION

Of fome General

POLITICAL RULES,

TO THE

PRESENT STATE

OF

GREAT-BRITAIN,

IRELAND AND AMERICA.

In a LETTER

To the Right Honourable EARL TEMPLE.

Clariffimi viri noftra civitatis temporibus optimis hoc fibi ampliffimum, pulcherrimumque ducebant, ab hofpitibus clientibufque fuis, ab exteris nationibus quæ in Amieftiam populi Romani ditionemque effent, injurias propulfare cerumque caufas defendere.

Cicero. Orat. Contra Cæcilium.

LONDON:

Printed for J. ALMON, oppofite Burlington-Houfe, in Piccadilly. 1766.

A N

APPLICATION, &c.

My Lord,

THE diffusive benevolence, and difinterefted deportment, which have characterifed your Lordfhip, through each private and public ftage of life, points you out as the perfon moft proper to be addreffed, by a man, who is willing to lay open fome errors in our policy, which require a fpeedy correction; you, my Lord, will extend your public concern beyond the confines of your native country, and confider every part of the human fpecies, which has any connection with England, as meriting your care and patronage.

There is not, perhaps, any one point of view, in which we can behold this kingdom at prefent more truly interefting, than that of the relation which it bears to thofe people, who are connected with us, in a fecondary *, or kind of dependant nature; fome

---

* Scotland without doubt, is united with England by the folemn act of both nations, but the fundametal difference of their laws is fo great, and their manners and ideas of government fo very difcordant, that I muft ftill behold them in the fecondary light in which it is placed above.

united,

united, but not receiving our municipal law, others receiving our laws after a ftruggle of many centuries, and others willing to make laws for themfelves, had they a power to execute them. After a war, therefore, in which a conftitutional exertion of our native ftrength has procured us at leaft a very refpectable commerce, nothing can more juftly merit our attention, than thofe nations, who, beyond the limits of England, form the feveral branches of the Britifh empire they are numerous, they inhabit countries abounding in all the neceffaries of life, and fruitful of the materials of many of its comforts; but above all, thefe countries produce the *genus acre virum marfam pubemque fabellam;* their cuftoms, nay, even their countenances, are Britifh, after a feries of generations; they have, in fhort, every title to the utmoft care and regard of the mother country, which intereft or affection fhould beftow.

The more heterogeneous the parts which enter into the compofition of any body, the lefs capable of folidity and permanency will it be; the jarring of their natures preventing that intimate union and firm cohefion, in which the ftrength of natural and of political bodies does primarily confift. This compactnefs, once attained to, good laws and inftitutions communicating their fpirit, give it that powerful momentum, which nothing can

can refift; if then a kingdom, from circumftances of colonization or otherwife, muft
have a connection with other people, it is
the duty and intereft of that kingdom to
affimilate thefe people with themfelves, as
foon as poffible; if to be born and fupported
by them, the nearer they are drawn like ar-
mour or garment, the lefs fenfible will the
principal be of the burthen; if able to fupport themfelves, perhaps affift the mother
country, the more clofely and naturally joined, the more capable like our limbs, will
they be to help and be of fervice; and yet
ftrange, although moft certain it is, that the
conquefts and colonies of nations, who themfelves have enjoyed Liberty, and are therefore more difcerning of the advantages which
it muft bring to others, have generally felt
more oppreffion, and have been lefs tenderly
cherifhed by the conquerors or colonizers,
than thofe of abfolute monarchies. Thus we
perceive, the conquered provinces of Rome,
far from being difpleafed * at the fall of the
commonwealth and eftablifhment of defpo-
tifm. Whether this arifes from the mean o-
pinion, which conquerors for the moft part
conceive of the conquered, deeming them
unworthy of, and incapable to make the proper ufe of Liberty, or from an hatred, im-

---

* *Neque provinciæ illum ftatum rerum abnuebans, fufpecto
fenatus populique imperio, ob certamina potentium et averitiam
magiftratum——*Tacit. 1. Annal.

preffed

preſſed by their obſtinacy when an enemy, I cannot determine : however, am inclined to believe, that upon the firſt reduction of them, the conquerors dared not truſt them with Liberty; but upon removal of theſe apprehenſions, by length of time and other circumſtances, they ceaſed to be actuated by the proper motive of conqueſt; the mighty maſters themſelves, degenerate and corrupt, loſe that benevolence which ſhould ſhare the bleſſings of a free government with their fellow creatures; nor are they impelled by a deſire of ſerving the human ſpecies, in being the inſtruments of the Almighty, in reſtoring it to the exerciſe of a rational, and ſince the goſpel diſpenſation, a chriſtian well-tempered Liberty : and this, with ſelf-defence, which ſuggeſts conqueſt by way of prevention *, are, in my opinion, the only principles upon which a conqueror can by any means whatſoever be juſtified. If they conſider the hearts of thoſe who have the misfortune of falling under their domination, as too narrow for the entertainment of the noble and elevated ſentiments of Liberty, and compare them to weak ſtomachs, which may be clogged and diſabled by ſolid and ſubſtantial food; or an eye, which long uſed to darkneſs, unexerciſed by real objects, nothing preſenting but figures and fantoms of

---

* *Cui poteſtas nocendi exipitur utiliter vincitur.*
Aug. de Civitate Dei.

its

its own creation, and which may be difor-
dered, perhaps deftroyed by too fudden an
infufion of a ftrong light; then fhould liberty
be portioned out to them by degrees, accord-
ing to a judicious and ftrict political regimen,
previous to which it is the duty of the conqueror to enlarge their underftandings, me-
liorate and prepare their hearts, for receiving
this plant of *cœleftial feed*; otherwife are
they left in a worfe condition than before,
and all the boafted encomiums of their
mafters upon liberty, and thofe bleffings which
their conftitution affords, are but blinds to
carry on their defigns, with vile views of
lawlefs dominion, and of a commerce whofe
objects are avarice and luxury.

To a perfon who confiders the ends of
conqueft in that extenfive, give me leave to
add moral and religious light, in which I am
well affured, that your Lordfhip beholds every
political matter; it muft be evident, from
the acknowledged goodnefs of the Creator,
that the happinefs of his creatures was the
end of their formation; and that in order to
give thefe creatures an oppportunity of rendering themfelves more gratetul to him, it
is placed within their power, by a proper
exercife of their faculty and freedom of
will, to be the meritorious inftruments of
making each other happy. One man has it
in his power to ferve his neighbour, the
neighbour gives his affiftance where it is
wanting:

wanting: one nation fupplies by commerce where another is defective, and is relieved in its turn : the conqueror gives to the conquered, arts, fciences, laws, manners; and receives from the conquered, numbers, friendfhip, additional ftrength; thereby forming a more powerful community, fecured againft external violence, quiet in the cultivation of ufeful knowledge, and in the practice of every moral virtue. It is difficult, I will confefs, for a people, who behold themfelves fuperior to others in arts, in arms and induftry, not to give way to an over favourable opinion of felf; and not to bear an haughtinefs of deportment to thofe, whom they look upon as fo far beneath them : this may be excufed, it is true, and charged to the account of human frailty in the uneducated, uninformed part of a people; even there, it were better if otherwife, and it is the duty of the leading men in fuch a ftate, carefully to fupprefs by authority and example every appearance of infolence; becaufe, no other things, not even fuperiority of wealth and power, can create fuch a degree of jealoufy in their neighbours; ftrangers wifh for an opportunity of humbling their pride ; their own provinces are at beft but indifferent whether they ftand or fall, and are often dubious, whether a change of mafter may not turn to their advantage. Surely then, my Lord, a nation happily circumftanced from fituation,

from

from climate, from a favourable temperature of mind and body, (all which unjuſtly attributed to chance, are produced by a chain of cauſes framed by providence for good and wiſe purpoſes) a nation thus diſtinguiſhed by heaven, ſhould not look upon theſe advantages as beſtowed merely for their own ſakes, and their effects to terminate within the narrow compaſs of England or of Italy; they ſhould behold themſelves in no other relation of ſuperiority, than as inſtruments of promoting real knowledge, pure religion, and virtuous liberty; the three moſt deſirable objects of human purſuit, and which perfected and refined form permanency, ſubſtantial, and rational happineſs. The power, therefore, which miſapplies advantages thus derived from the ſupreme Being for the above purpoſes; who thinks each country, whoſe inhabitants they can out-number or out-diſcipline, a new ſource of luxury to their diſſipated, effeminate, immoral nobility and gentry; who treat their allies and colonies as miniſters only to their pleaſures and profuſions; the dominion of ſuch a people can be but of ſhort duration; becauſe its exiſtence, and the general ſcheme of providence, are incompatible: their inſolence confirms them that other countries are made for their ſole uſe and gratification; this leads to luxury, to debility, to ſecurity; ſo by natural cauſes, as clear as the laws of motion to the man
who

who clofely obferves the political effects,
which gradations to vice in thofe individuals conftituting a community, have always
produced ; this nation's ruin muft be acce-
lerated : it muft give way to fuperior virtue ;
from which a completion of the defigns of
providence may with more reafon be expected. Thefe ideas of the ends of conqueft,
however ill fuited to the refinement of the
age we live in, may I doubt not ftand the
violence of modern ridicule, if fortunate
enough to merit your Lordfhip's fanction ;
and here, however diffatisfied with myfelf,
when varying in opinion from fo refpectable
a writer as the Baron Montefquieu, yet
muft I declare, that the applaufe beftowed
upon the fpirit, with which Alexander conquered the Perfian empire, by that great
politician, feems founded upon notions of
conqueft, which arife rather from falfe
glory and oftentation, than any real utility
to the human fpecies ; elfe would he never
have panygerized that hero for renouncing
the fober, manly, virtuous manners of
Greece, and adopting the foft and luxurious
manners of Perfia ; and to what end ? why,
thro' an excefs of tendernefs to the vanquifh-
ed. This I will venture to fay may be better
accounted for by the fudden turn to pleafure,
which that young hero had taken, and his
love for the fair Afiatick princefs, than upon
any principles of uncommon humanity ; and
it

it is fubmitted to your lordfhip, whether his
humanity would not have difplayed itfelf to
greater advantage, by bringing over the Per-
fians to the difcipline of his own country :
it being moft certain, as he himfelf has obferved, that fuch nations, as have the misfortune to be conquered, are for the moft
part degenerated from their original inftitutions *, rather ferved by deftroying their
pernicious prejudices, and laid by conqueft
under an happier genius ; fo that leaving a
nation to its own bad laws and cuftoms,
which are often a difgrace to humanity, is
like leaving a wayward child to its own bad
humours, when wholfome correction fhould
be adminiftred, in order to reform a nature,
perhaps originally vicious (being born in fin;)
and as it is the duty of a parent, whom experience, education, and a mild and moral religion
has qualified for the tafk, to beftow them on
his offspring ; nay, to ufe feverity, if found
reluctant to his difcipline : fo is it of a con-
quering nation, enlightened by literature and
pure chriftianity, to offer to the conquered a
better fet of manners than their own ; and
if rejected, by proper political conftraints,
where the idea of cruelty is totally excluded,
compel to receive them, and become happy.

The moderns, to whom chriftianity has
given great advantage over the antients in that

C   article

---

* Montefquieu l'efprit d'loix, lib. 10. chap. 14.

article of rendering fervice to human nature, by their power and influence, have pro-
pagated their religion, I mean the Catholick
fect, with a view only to empire and profit : they propagate religion with a defign
of making it, by the affiftance of their
priefts, an engine of dominion, rather than
a *light to enlighten the Gentiles* ; and infufe fo
poifonous a mixture of wicked and fuperfti-
tious prejudices into the chalice, which they
prefent to the innocent deluded natives,
whom they have fubdued, or fet down
amongft ; that inftead of being invigorated
and filled with the fpirit to perform good
and chriftian works, they become intoxicated
by the draught, and are entirely loft to any
notion of the charities. The Proteftants
agree in confidering trade as their ultimate ;
but in matters of religion are fo cool and
indifferent (except in one of our American
colonies) that they look upon religion as a
plant, which muft rear itfelf for them, or
abfolutely perifh, and fcandaloufly remifs in
the bufinefs of reclaiming their favage fellow-creatures, to which end alone providence
has vefted them with fuch ample powers,
think themfelves totally acquitted of doing
no fort of good by the aid of religion, they
can withhold themfelves from making it the
inftrument of evil. Such is the abufe of
thefe advantages, by the nations of Europe
who are favoured by heaven, and as it were
intrufted

intrufted with the care and inftruction of the yet uncivilized part of the globe. The Jews, once a chofen people of the Deity, perverfly refufed the light of the gofpel when offered ; the nations of chriftendom, who feem elected to be the difpenfers of the true religion, either neglect to let in the light upon their fellow-creatures, or throw in fuch a glare of fuperftiticus pageantry, as muft dazzle, or entirely darken their underftandings.

It is not pretended, that when enterprizes are fet on foot, when difcoveries of new countries are propofed, that undertakers can be fufficiently animated by the deliberate moral motive which I have infifted upon. Velofco d' Gama, with the other Portugueze adventurers upon the coaft of Africa, whilft they were erecting croffes wherever they landed in honour of chriftianity, by the acknowledgment of their own hiftorian, De Feria, received the real fpur to enterprize from a defire of gold, and other materials of trade: as did, with fome addition of a love of fame and glory, the Englifh navigators, Raleigh, Drake, and others. The thoughtlefs feaman and foldier, muft have a mere fenfual object for his end. But it is the duty of the cool fpeculative ftatefman, to dart his eye beyond the furface ; and to manage in fuch a manner, that not only his own country, but the human fpecies, fhall

receive

receive moral benefit, from the paffions and propenfities of individuals.

The general obligation by which the civilized parts of the globe are bound to communicate morality, religion, arts and fciences to the reft, and confequently liberty the root of all, (for abfolute conftraint even to good, puts a negative upon any merit in the action;) I fay, my Lord, this general obligation had almoft drawn me from fight of my particular fubject, which was contracted to the ideas of that bad policy in free ftates, which have treated their allies or colonies with feverity; who have been remifs in preparing them for liberty, and when prepared, who have refufed to beftow it on them.

The Romans were brave, they were wife (in fpite of Grecian romance), they were virtuous above all other nations; yet were they far from perfection in that part of their policy which related to their allies. It is not the lot of mortals. They entertained notions too exalted of their own merit; and it was with great reluctance, that their neighbours were received into any kind of equality with them; witnefs the indifference of Romulus, in revenging the death of Tatius *, upon the Laurentes, which had a
face

---

* Eam rem minus agre quam dignum erat tuliffe Romulum ferunt, feu ob infidam focietatem regni, &c.
poft

face of connivance, if not of having been an accomplice in the murder. The vigour, indeed, and courage, with which the Samnites and other Italian ftates fo long defended their independency, was enough to create a jealoufy in the minds of the Romans; and we therefore fee that it was not, until enemies of greater fize and danger had obliged them to form their armies out of thefe ftates, that this jealoufy abated. Yet, to the laft, the center being the poft of ftrength, always confilting of the legions and the allies, placed upon the flanks; this military inftitution, rigidly obferved, prove, that they continued to entertain fome doubts, either of the fidelity or capacity of their conquered friends. But as luxury encreafed, and the apprehenfion of foreign enemies vanifhed, their antipathy to the allies became more vifible; all notions of that equality, fo effential to the very being of republicks, was intolerable; and lords of the world themfelves, they would lord it over thofe who fo powerfully contributed to make them fo; arrogating the merit of every acquifition made by the ftates: the profits they alfo feized upon, by monopolizing the conquered lands, in direct oppofi-

---

poft Tatii mortem ab fua parte non erat regnatum in focietate aqua.

Romani veteres peregrinum regem afpernabantur, liv. 1.

oppofition to the old, but not abrogated Licinian law. Thus would they exalt themfelves above their fellow foldiers, for no other reafon, that we can difcover, but that of being born nearer the Tyber, or within fight of the Capitol. The allies were difgufted, and with reafon; the Mani, the Peligni, over whom, or without whofe affiftance Rome never had triumphed, beheld thefe acts of infolence with the warmeft indignation; they demanded that freedom of the city, to which their fervices had intitled them; they were fupported in thefe demands by Mummius *, Beftia, Cotta, fome of the moft refpectable names of Rome; the fecond Africanus, who was an eye-witnefs of their bravery, affifted them with his credit and intereft, and loft his popularity amongft the old citizens, by an act of the greateft equity. Thefe laft the Patricians had gained, by raifing jealoufies in their minds againft the allies and their abettors, and were moft effectually fupported by the order of knights, at that time the moft profligate body of men that ever difgraced a community; yet, formidable in the poffeffion of a judicial power in cafes of bribery, corruption, and mifbehaviour in publick office. What the allies could not obtain by the interceffion of fuch

* Vide Appian, on the civil wars of Rome, where he treats of the caufes of the focial war.

great

great and virtuous men, they fought by force.
A war broke out; the greateft Roman gene-
rals, Sextus, Cæfar, Craffus, even Sylla and
Marius, yielded in their turns to the bravery
and conduct of a Judacilius, an Egnatius, a
Cato; fo bloody was the war on the fide of
Rome, as to produce an ordinance, that the
killed in battle fhould be buried on the fpot,
and not brought into the city, left the
numbers of dead bodies fhould intimidate
the people; they armed their freedmen, a
ftep never taken, but in cafes of the greateft
emergency. At length, obliged to divide
the allies, they granted to thofe, who had not
appeared in arms, the freedom of the city;
by this ftroke of policy did they confirm the
wavering, give hopes to thofe who had de-
clared againft them, of obtaining the fame,
loofened the ties of the confederacy, and
blunted, in a great meafure, the edge of a-
nimofity. From the day on which the Julian
Law was paffed (called fo from Sextus Julius
Cæfar, who enacted it) the arms of the republick were more profperous. However,
the war continued even under thefe circumftances of disjunction, fo unfavourable to the
allies, until they carried their point; and all
the Italian ftates, the Lucanians and Samnites themfelves, names hateful, and let me
add, terrible to the Romans, were at length
admitted to their freedom.

Thus

Thus, my Lord, does it appear how fatal the pride, the avarice, the ambition, the arrogance of Rome, had nearly proved to the very being of their commonwealth ; how an affectation of being select, how a difdain to mix, to incorporate with their countrymen, and thereby to ſtrengthen the whole, had almoſt produced a total obliteration of the Roman name ; and how Rome, by diſregarding theſe ends of conqueſts, for which I have before contended, by endeavouring to engroſs all, were put to the utmoſt ſtretch of policy to fecure any. If the Romans had frankly ſhared their privileges with the allies, upon the footing they afterwards granted them, had they done it with an air of good-will, then would they have avoided this dreadful war; and the new citizens entertain no diſtinction in their minds between themſelves and the old citizens, they would have confidered the riches, the ſplendor, the glory of Rome as their own ; they would feel her misfortunes, and rejoice in her proſperity ; and they would have maintained a ſuperiority in the love, gratitude, and refpect of the new citizens, though not by the laws and conſtitution : in ſhort, the allies would ſuffer Rome to govern, but not admit her right of doing ſo. But the very bad grace with which theſe immunities were ceded, extorted as it were by force, a feries of indignities; ſuch as turning them out of the city during the

the time of elections, with the ftrongeft ex-
preffions of contempt, had fo difgufted thefe
high-fpirited people, and fo alienated their
hearts from their fellow citizens, that we
behold them ever afterwards ftimulated by a
remembrance of fuch fevere treatment, to
give their votes againft the Patrician party,
whether in the right or in the wrong, and
forced into the arms of every ambitious dif-
turber of the public tranquility. I will admit, that the party of whom I now fpeak,
did in the end, by fupporting Cæfar, rivet
the chains of Roman flavery; yet muft it be
infifted upon, that the proud Patrician did
kindle and blow up that fire in which thefe
chains were forged; they who fhould have
wifdom to forefee the bad effects of injuring
a brave people, in whom moderation fhould
have been a check upon avarice and infolence, whofe fagacity fhould have pointed
out to them, how unreafonable that they alone
fhould fhare the conquered lands, and enjoy
the fpoils of a plundered world. Men who
would not fee thefe things, could not with
reafon complain, if thofe who fuffered this
unjuft exclufion from their immunities and
rights, were not fo philofophically temperate,
as to be always in an humour to forgive and
reject every preferred occafion of being re-
venged. Who, my Lord, fhould be wife in
a country, if that body of men are not fo,
whofe fortunes, whofe ftations, furnifh lei-

fure,

fure, with all the other means of acquiring ufeful knowledge, and of improving their natural talents to the utmoft perfection of which they are capable? To what end the difference of wealth and power between them, and any other two legged animal in the community? Why that difference maintained by this community, unlefs for the good of the whole? God never gives fo unequally for the poffeffor's fake; he defigns this inequality as the root from which that fubordination fprings, which is to produce publick convenience and tranquility. Should not then thefe men, in whofe power it is fo happily placed to fubdue their paffions and refine their natures, avoid every occafion of raifing animofity and difguft in the minds of their countrymen? Should it not be rather their glory to bear with their intemperance? This furely is more commendable, than to practife upon their weaknefs, wanton in their misfortunes, and inftead of lightening, add to that burthen, which their fuperiority muft always lay upon a people whofe labour and induftry muft fupport it.

The Italian allies were never wanting in refpect to Rome; even when brought to the loweft extremity by Annibal, very few of them having joined the Carthaginians from choice; Capua, indeed, fo naturally difpofed to vice, that fhe outran her miftrefs by at leaft a century in the race of corruption.

tion. She it is true moſt cordially went over to the enemy; but in general, conſidering the great diſtreſſes of the commonwealth, the faith of the allies was wonderful; and tho' keeping pace with Rome in all her conqueſts, ſuch was their modeſty, as never to think themſelves on a level with that metropolis, until her citizens were fallen from virtue. They acknowledged her ſuperiority, till ſhe no longer knew how to govern herſelf; and when the ſtates of Italy had arrived at an equal perfection with the Romans in arts, in ſciences, in arms; when their manners were the ſame, their ideas of liberty as inlarged; when their language yielded not to that of Rome, except, perhaps, in ſmartneſs of pronunciation, or ſome quaint turn of phraſe; when their ſtrength of numbers to be employed in extending their conqueſts, or ſecuring thoſe already made, were by no means inferior; why ſhould they not be admitted to a ſhare of government? Why not enjoy the fruits of their toil and hazard? Why not be intruſted with the care of Italy, of their own liberties and properties? It is not from being born within the ſame narrow diſtrict that the identity of country ariſes? Country, in the great ſenſe of the word, admits no limitation from extent of territory, or number; none but want of contiguity, want of a ſimilitude of manners, intereſts, and objects of hap-

pineſs

pinefs impofe ; for thefe are wants which
may caufe an unweildinefs in exercifing the
members of the political body; to feel for
the fafety, the profperity, the glory and liberty of the fame country, is what confti-
tutes us countrymen and fellow citizens :
the fafety of the Roman name, its laws,
its cuftoms, wherever difperfed by colony, or
otherwife, was the care of every Italian at
the period I now fpeak of; and he who
had thefe warmly at heart, was furely en-
titled to all the privileges of a Roman citi-
zen. Had it been the evil fortune of Rome
to have Carthage or Macedon to contend
with, when they had fo unreafonably pro-
voked their allies; what a weight would
thefe warlike nations have thrown into the
fcale of the enemy; they would have felt as
forely as Carthage did from the refentment
of their abfurd African neighbours. Happily for them no combination was able, at
that time, to ftand before that plan of power
which their virtuous anceftors had formed.
The civilized part of the world, Afia and
Greece, were impatient of the yoke, but
abject and enervated ; nor had the northern
nations entered into thefe defenfive affocia-
tions, which foon becoming offenfive ter-
minated in the deftruction of Roman tyranny. Europe was not at that time digefted
into ftates, whofe fmaller policies bore a refpect to the grand policy of the whole; it
did

did not fhare one common military difcipline as at prefent; nor was every country watchful and attentive to each movement of its neighbour; no compacts made for checking the growth and profperity of any power which was hated or feared. Had that been the cafe, the Roman fenate would never have given caufe of complaint to their fubjects; on the contrary, it would have grappled them clofer by every endearment of friendfhip and affection; and altho' loft to virtue and found policy, Rome would have regarded its prefent immediate intereft and prefervation, and never difobliged a people, whom nature, by proximity and other circumftances, had deftined to be a part of themfelves.

There are no hiftorical corollaries more certain, than that all ftates, who have extended their empire by colony or conqueft, and who are not difpofed to unite thefe countries with themfelves after a fufficient preparation, muft employ governors in thefe countries whofe every motion cannot be clofely watched; that as the principal country comes to lofe its virtues, an indifference, at leaft, about the intereft of provinces muft enfue.

That thefe governors are feldom troubled with any infpection of their conduct, or any after-reckoning; becaufe each leading man, expecting one time or other to exercife the

fame office, in order to fecure himfelf againft
future punifhment, will not eftablifh a pre-
cedent againft himfelf by condemning another : thus emancipated from fear, each governor improves in the abufe of power, until
a fyftem of abufe comes at length to be
finifhed and entire ; and this is handed
down as a rule of government to all who
fucceed to the office ; they wifh not to a-
mend the laws of the province, nor the
manners of the natives ; they plunder the
inhabitants under the cover of laws, to which
by an artful delufion they are brought to give
their affent ; for they enter into a compofition with fome of the principals of the
country, who by a fmooth addrefs, and the
fly arts of popularity, find means to glide
into the eafy confidence of the people ; and
thefe, in confideration of a very trifling part
of the fpoil yielded to them by their
haughty employer, undergo the drudgery of
fecuring the reft to him.

Rome, the authority to which I fhall ever
recur in political reflections upon free ftates,
(for to trace out the mind of man in the
hiftory of arbitrary governments, where each
individual acts under conftraint, would be
to delineate the movements of the human
body, from obfervations made upon con-
vulfionaries.) Rome furnifhes many inftances
of governors, prætors, proconfuls, who have
fcandaloufly pillaged the unhappy provinces
com-

committed to their charge ; and it abounds with inftances of a fhameful failure of juftice, when thefe delinquents have been impeached by the deputies * from the provinces ; it was upon the acquittal of Cotta Salinator, and Manlius Aquileius himfelf by the fenate, and this in direct contradiction to the ftrongeft evidence of guilt, that the cognizance of the crimes of extortion, and others of a public nature, was transferred from the Patricians to the order of knights ; and tho' an infttution of the younger Gracchus, yet do we find Cicero † lamenting the revival of this part of the fenatorial jurifdiction, by Sylla. In fuch low eftimation was the juftice of a Roman Senate at that time ; and fuch an intereft had Verres eftablifhed by the force of gold, that if the zeal and great talent of Cicero had not fo powerfully interfered, bribery, together with the proftitute eloquence of Hortenfius, would

---

* If the people of Sicily had been reprefented in a gegeneral affembly, it is probable that Verres would have efcaped unpunifhed, as his money might have procured him a majority in that affembly to fanctify his conduct ; but unfortunately for him, each city had its affembly and a power of remonftrating fingly before a Roman Senate ; nor could fuch a wealthy, ufeful town as Manchefter be precluded from juftice by the vote of a corrupt reprefentative of an old Sarum.

† Judiciorum levitate ordo quoque alius ad res judicandas requiritur. Oratio contra Cœcelium.

would have procured him his own friend Cœci-
lius for his accufer, who was, without doubt,
an accomplice in his villainies : fo difficult
is the tafk of keeping governors of provinces
within the bounds of duty; fo difficult to
find a tribunal, whofe integrity fhall anfwer
to fo arduous a tafk ! But when we confider
how much further than the particular fuf-
ferings and difcontents of the province,
the certain bad effects of an unjuft, rapa-
cious conduct of the governors of provinces
muft be felt, our apprehenfions for the
fafety of the principal country takes the
alarm ; when we confider that thefe governments afford the moft plentiful fources of
luxury; that the means of gratifying the
ambition of private men, nay, that ambition itfelf has for the moft part its origin,
in elevating and habituating any member of
a community to a kind of temporary dominion, as viceroy or procunful; when we re-
flect upon the number of bad fubjects, of
wicked doftroyers, of public tranquillity or
liberty, which has been made by a fatal
exaltation of individuals in free ftates;
we cannot hefitate one moment, in determining to fupprefs every neceffity of raifing
a fubject to a condition, in which he might
believe himfelf a king; and to cut him off
from any opportunity of amaffing fuch fuperior wealth, as may, by bribes or evil example, enable him to debauch the morals,
and

and deſtroy the love of liberty in his fellow-citizens. It was not until Cæſar had been ten years at the head of legions in Gaul, that he diſdained to bear a ſuperior in the common-wealth ; he never would have plunged into a debt of 170,000l. had he not the hopes of repairing his ſhattered fortunes by the plunder of ſome rich province; and without the plunder of his province he never would be able to bring over the tribes to his intereſt, and influence all elections ; ſo far removed as he was from the ſcene of intrigue; and if it was not for the unmerited honours heaped upon Pompey, the ſcandalous adulation of the Patricians, and the amazing power conferred upon him in the war of the Pirates, he too might have endured an equal in the common-wealth. In ſhort, my Lord, it requires, I am ſure, ſomething more than modern virtue to ſtand againſt the intoxication of power, to look with temperance upon great wealth, and not to apply that wealth, when occaſion ſhall preſent, in obtaining an unconſtitutional influence in a free ſtate ; it muſt then of conſequence be the duty of legiſlature, to reduce the means of acquiring diſproportionate wealth, or alarming power, which cannot be better effected, than by conſolidating, as far as circumſtances will admit, all the parts of an empire ; this will ſupercede the neceſſity of many governors,

E   who,

who, unable to reconcile themfelves to that face of equality which liberty requires, are wonderfully zealous to work its total deftruction ; and this palpable advantage muft follow, that when the parts of an empire have all the fame legiflative as well as executive government, the intercourfe between the head and the members will be more lively, and things will not pafs thro' the medium of corrupt, indolent, or ignorant viceroys, where truth meets with many delays, and is oftentimes totally obftructed.

Contiguity of fituation, or a ftrong likenefs of manners and cuftoms, one of which nature alone can furnifh, the other attainable to by political induftry and addrefs ; either of thefe are fo powerfully effential to union, that without one or the other, it is not fuppofed that union can poffibly take place ; and when union has taken place, it never fhould be clogged by partial circumftances, but be as entire as poffible ; otherwife it will be a caufe of weaknefs, and not of ftrength. To apply thefe doctrines, firft to the cafe of Scotland, from the acceffion of James the fixth of Scotland to the throne of England, until the folemn act of union. Scotland bore the fame relation to England, that the ftates of Italy did to Rome, before the focial war had produced a grant of the immunities of the city to thefe ftates, and altho' the Britifh union was not obtained by
force

force as was that of Italy, yet the apprehenfions (during a bloody war with France,
a pretender to the Britifh crown in being,
ftrongly fupported by the moft enterprizing
prince in Europe ;) of thofe Highlanders
whom Godolphin had armed, did certainly
determine that minifter to bring about an
union, and thereby remove all danger from
that quarter ; fo that neither the Italian nor
Britifh union was the effect of mutual good
will; exclufive of other motives, we fee
convenience, prefent expediency, and feveral other caufes interfere : be that as it
will, the event having taken place, all meafures for producing that likenefs and cordiality, which is the ftrongeft political band,
fhould be purfued by every honeft man ; and
to this we are warmly admonifhed by the
example of Rome, where a want of affection between the new and old citizens threw
the weight of the former into the fcale
of every corrupt party which arofe in the
ftate, and attached them, not to their country, but to a Marius, a Cinna, or a Cæfar.

Had the fame gothick fpirit prevailed,
which made wars and conquefts the fole end
of taking up arms, then may it with injuftice be faid (however parradoxical it fhould
appear) that Scotland, in a ftate of feparation
from England would be more ufeful than
united as at prefent ; for it would have kept

England alert, and attentive to war. The privileges enjoyed by the inhabitants of the marches, shewing how neceſſary their preſence to guard our frontier againſt this warlike neighbour. But England, ſecured from the north-eaſt by the declenſion of the Daniſh power; and having a barrier to the ſouth, in its poſſeſſions upon the Continent ; would have ſunk into * indolence and effeminacy, had they no enemies within the iſland ; and it is to their wars with the Scotch and Welch, that they owe the bravery and diſcipline of thoſe armies, which throw ſuch a luſtre upon the reigns of our Edwards and Henries, by their glorious atchivements in France. England, as well as all Europe, is very differently circumſtanced from what they were in the days of our plantagenets ; the ſpirit of our age is truly commercial ; the advantages thence ariſing, are found to be more real and ſubſtantial than the glare, the tumult of conqueſt and triumph. War, from being conſidered as an end, is happily dwindled into the means ; and nations, when they conquer, do it rather with an eye to repriſal or diverſion, than with a deſign of retaining the conqueſt. Our great extent of coaſt,

---

* Is hoſtis velut natus ad continendam inter magnorum intervalla bellorum Romanis militarem diſciplinam erat: nec deerat unquam cum iis vel materia belli, vel cauſa; quia propter domeſticam inopiam vicinos agros incurſabant, Liv. lib. 39.

our

our luxuriant produ&ion of all the capital
materials of trade, form a ſtronger commercial incentive than any of our neighbours
can feel. If Scotland, then, inſtead of being united with us, ſtood conne&ed with
France by alliances founded in the early periods, upon reaſon and ſelf-preſervation, engaged by her intereſt to be ever ready in
joining to reduce the ſtrength of her formidable neighbour, ſhe would be able moſt
powerfully to divert our attention from ma-
nufa&ures, from exportations, and our navy;
not having within herſelf many inducements
to commerce, war would be her trade, as it
is that of Germany ; and it is evident from
the great ſucceſs of Pruſſia againſt the Houſe
of Auſtria, how ſmall a number of inhabitants whoſe reigning paſſion is for war, may
furniſh matter of heavy embarraſment to a
very numerous and wealthy people. Yet,
ſenſible as I am of the great advantage it
muſt be, both to Scotland and England, that
their union ſhould be cloſe, cordial, free
from all jarrings and jealouſies as poſſible,
ſtill muſt I ſpeak with freedom ſome thoughts
which ariſe, not from want of a due regard
to the merit of that country, but with a view
to reduce pride, vanity, prejudice, or whatever
elſe may obſtru& that ſalutary ſcheme of
cloſe friendſhip, which is indiſputably the
intereſt of the whole iſland—Firſt of all, I
am far from conſidering that people, however

ever refpectable the individuals may be for their prudence and perfonal bravery, in fo principal a view as their own writers are pleafed to do, and amongft the reft, the author of an extraordinary paper, dated at Edinburgh. Writers of the polemical clafs, feel a higher glow of imagination than can be uniformly confiftent with ftrict truth; paffion and party are apt to raife their colourings fomewhat higher than any thing we behold in nature. Scotland, from its contracted territory, poverty of foil, and fmall number of inhabitants, was ever under the neceffity of reforting to a foreign alliance, in order to procure to themfelves, as a people, any degree of confequence : as an enemy, they muft be looked upon, therefore, in a fecondary light, they are not in the fame rank with the Gaul and Carthaginian, but to the Samnite, may they with great juftice be compared. Their alliances with Ireland, enabled them to difturb the ancient South Britons, and alarm the Romans when fettled in this ifland. But, it is well known, that fince the coming in of our Saxon anceftors, with the trifling number of 1600 men, to the aid of Vortigern, againft the Picts, the Northern Britons *, never prefumed to do

more

* As to my purpofe, it is quite indifferent whether the prefent Scotch, are a mix'd breed of Picts and Scotch, or whether the Picts were totally eradicated, fince both were equally

more than peep into England, until the Norman conqueſt; when the Engliſh, who were ſtripped of their eſtates by William the firſt, carried their diſcontents into Scotland, and and encouraged that people to reaſſume their diſorderly inroads into Northumberland. Our poſſeſſions upon the continent, fixed a kind of natural enemy in the king of France, to whom the Scotch very politically attached themſelves, and drew from that ſource a conſideration, to which they could not otherwiſe poſſibly attain; and when we conſider the Engliſh as a people compounded of Saxons and of Normans, deſcended on one ſide from nations who had deſtroyed the moſt powerful empire the world ever beheld, whoſe name alone was ſufficient to retain the Pict within bounds; and who ſo bravely withſtood the Daniſh force, not the attacks of roving pirates, as is vulgarly ſuppoſed, but a ſteady, well conducted, invaſive war, ſupported by the maritime powers who inhabited the northern coaſt of Europe, from the mouth of the Elbe, and ſo along both ſhores of the Baltick; when we view them deſcended, on the other ſide, from Nor-

---

equally terrified by the Saxon power; during ſome of the diſtractions of the heptarchy, they ſometimes ventured into Northumberland; and once leaguing with the South Britains, under their king Aidan, they were for a moment ſucceſsful againſt Ceaulin king of Weſſex. |

mans,

mans, the conquerors of the fineſt province in France, and eſtabliſhing kingdoms, at their will, through Europe; when we conſider themſelves the poſterity of theſe celebrated nations, as the conquerors of all France, and arbiters of Europe, abſurd and ridiculous muſt be that degree of vanity, which aſſumes any pretenſions of ſuperiority, in valour, or any other ſpecies of merit, over ſuch a people.

But as to notions of civil liberty, for which that writer appears ſo much to have valued them, it is in that point, I think them principally defective : love of liberty does not entirely conſiſt in reſolving to maintain independency of a foreign power, there are many other eſſentials to a true love of liberty ; becauſe, a nation may be very free from any influence from abroad, and yet totally enſlaved at home ; the lords and leading men of ſuch nation, may labour to guard their country againſt ſtrangers, with no other deſign, but that of ſecuring the benefit of its vaſſalage to themſelves; ſo that publick ſpirit, may poſſibly have no concern whatſoever in any of their actions; and really, if any thing can ſink the Scottiſh nation ſo low, as inaptitude for a compleat junction with England, it is the little reliſh they have ever ſhewn for the true bleſſings of liberty. He who would infer the contrary, from the reſiſtance ſo often given to
their

their kings, would make the moſt fallacious inference in the world ; for many oppoſitions to kings, have proceeded from a partiality to the domination of the heads of clans, the worſt ſpecies of ſlavery, and not from any deſire of being free. Scotland has deſtroyed many of its kings, it is granted, but not with an eye to promote the cauſe of liberty ; let it appear, that the Scottiſh inſurrection had ever any ſuch tendency ; that they ever attempted to diſcharge, from the minds of the people, their ſlaviſh prejudices, or ſtupid adoration of their lairds, that they ever wiſhed the bleſſing of liberty ſhould extend to every individual who deſerved it ; in ſhort, that previous to the union, they ever ſeriouſly thought of deſtroying their heritable juriſdictions ; let theſe appear, and Scotland's claim to a love of liberty, ſhall, with her many other well-grounded claims to merit, be moſt willingly admitted.

Reaſons may be drawn from the original formation of the Scottiſh government, why they have been particularly ſlow in their approaches to liberty ; but ſome obſervations upon government in general, and upon the difference between the old and more modern Celtick forms in particular, muſt neceſſarily be promiſed. The end of ſocial aſſociation, is the preſervation of thoſe individuals who compoſe it ; in a ſtate of nature, the preſervation of ſingle ſelf is the

F ; ſole

sole object; no regard to numbers or country, is suppofed to countervail this firft confideration; we, in that ftate, owe nothing
to numbers or country, and nothing will
we pay. But from the moment that a community is eftablifhed, to felf-defence, as a
primary object*, that of a nation or aggra-
gate of individuals is fubftituted; and it is
not from the good of any particular, but
from the good of the whole, that the rule of
action muft arife. In this ftate of fociety,
the idea of prefervation, from being more
extended, becomes more complicated and
difficult; and to thofe who do not ferioufly
attend to the ends of government, and the
fubftitution of that general good which has
taken place, to the particular good which
before prevailed; fingle felf-prefervation, is
ever prefling upon their minds; and cafes
frequently arife, where partiality to felf, and
inattention to publick order and convenience,
hinder us from acquiefcing, but with reluctance and diffatisfaction, under the moft
wholefome regulations. In general, the rea-
fonablenefs of giving up our private opinion,
though we fhould fuftain a damage, is pretty
apparent; but fome particular incidents there
muft be, where it is not fo apparent; for
inftance, where the dignity of the executive

---

* For though felf-prefervation is the firft law of nature,
it is not fo of fociety.

power

power of a ſtate, ſeems not to conſiſt with
the civil liberty of the ſubjcct; here the
wiſdom and penetration of the expounders of
law is called forth ; here the arduous taſk of
ſecuring a part from ſuffering, without en-
dangering the whole ; and the important
queſtion comes into agitation ; Whether the
luxuriancies of liberty, wild and beautiful as
they appear, but often pernicious to the
fruit of good government, ſhail be lopped
and kept under ? Or whether too great a
hazard of deſtroying the ſtock, may not enſue the operation, and ſome abuſes of liberty
be more prudently ſubmitted to, than mea-
ſures taken, by which its entire ruin, even
by the moſt remote poſſibility, may be in-
curred ? This laſt, is certainly the ſpirit of
our law, and it places liberty amongſt thoſe
things which it is moſt inclined to favour,
looking upon it with a fond parental eye, as
that darling child, to whoſe advantage every
preſumption is admitted, every conſtruction
made, rather than ſee it ſo culpable, as to
merit a correction which may by any means
injure its beloved frame. That form therefore
of government, which provides moſt effectually for the liberty of the individual,
without weakening the ſtrength of the ma-
giſtrate ; that form which ſecures the greateſt number, or proportion, of its ſubjects
againſt internal oppreſſion, as well as external violence, is undoubtedly the beſt, be-

cauſe

cause it establishes order and safety, the great ends for which we enter into a state of society, at the expence of a very moderate share of that liberty, which we enjoy in a state of nature; and confers great social advantages, while it deprives us of very few natural ones. No liberty whatsoever can compensate the want of security in a state of nature; the hourly apprehensions of superior force; the inquietudes, which are the perpetual attendants upon fear; defence must be small, because every man rests his reservation upon his own powers; hence, we behold savages always improving their bodily strength, increasing their agility, acquiring the greatest possible degree of swiftness, and practising patience under labour and fatigue; insomuch, that the American Aborigines, are said almost to fly over continents, lie whole nights in snow, and perform such feats as seem almost incredible; relying on single self for their preservation. With regard to parental government, this, as it is extremely defective in point of defence, however mild and gentle it may be, from the affectionate relation between the governor and governed, being his offspring, so is it little to my present purpose; I shall, therefore, pass to those Celtic forms, which furnish the original materials of all the European constitutions. There are distinguished in history, two grand emigrations of those northern

northern people, whom all writers agree to
be Celtic; and each emigration made an at-
tack upon the Roman empire: in the firſt,
they were at length repulſed; in the latter,
they ſucceeded, and laid the foundation of
all the European kingdoms as above. The
firſt adventurers, obliged at length to aban-
don Italy, ſpread themſelves over Gaul, the
northern parts of Spain, Britain, and very
probably made ſome ſettlements in Ireland.
They left their mother country poſſeſſed
with the ſame ſpirit of conqueſt, which
actuated the Goths, Vandals, Alans, &c.
and the neceſſity of acquiring a ſettlement,
(there being no room, as is ſuppoſed, for
them at home) eſtabliſhed a ſtrict diſcipline
and due ſubordination; a reſpect to one ſuperior, kept every ſmall chief to his duty,
and prevented thoſe broils and diſſentions,
which ever ſince the ſiege of Troy, have retarded the progreſs of great enterprizes,
where they have been ſuffered to interfere.
But, my Lord, why the Goths, Vandals,
&c. had the good fortune to eſtabliſh more
excellent, and for that reaſon, more perma-
nent governments, than the conquerers of
the more early period, may appear from a
conſideration of the great difference in the
circumſtances of the invaded nations at the
different periods. The laſt emigrants fell
upon the ſouth of Europe, at a time when
the Roman laws, inſtitutions, arts and ſciences,

ces, had univerfally taken place ; and altho'
they conquered, yet, had they much to ap-
prehend from a people who were in poffeffion of that difcipline, which had fubdued
the world. In fome countries, their conquefts were fo imperfect, that they were
conftrained to a compofition with the inhabitants, and to take but part of their lands,
and part of their flaves ; they were, for this
reafon, obliged to have a watchful eye upon
enemies fo refpectable, and adhere to thofe
principles of policy, which they brought
from their own country. Hence, thofe
powerful mixed monarchies which we have
fince beheld in Europe ; fome few flourifhing
and vigorous, at the time others languid, de-
clining, and fcarce difcoverable to be of the
Gothick kind. The more early Celtes, met
with a different reception when they marched
to the fouthward ; for Roman virtue having
forced them over the Alps, they fell upon
nations who afforded them an eafy conqueft ;
and for whom, the facility of the conqueft,
muft infpire them with contempt ; they foon
became eafy, indolent, and fecure ; loft fight
of their ancient inftitutions ; no regard to a
general intereft ; each petty leader purfuing
a felfifh, narrow plan ; and hence the imper-
fection of thefe governments, which Cæfar
and Tacitus defcribe, both in Gaul and Britain. Nations, whofe want of political ce-
ment, rather than of weight or numbers,

was

was the caufe why they were immediately overturned by the Roman armies; whom, even their enemies allow to have been brave, but divided into fuch little ftates, that thefe divifions, and the want of a more comprehenfive band of union, did certainly produce their ruin. There can be no doubt, but the Scotch government is derived from the Celtick confined fountain, and has drawn from thence, the many imperfections with which it abounds; their leaders of clans, the unnatural diftinction between people of one fept, from thofe of another, yet both living in the fame country; the cruel animofity between thefe different fepts; (fo cruel, that inftances have appeared, where but one man alone, out of a name confifting of 2000, has furvived the rage of the adverfe clan, and all this to gratify the paltry ambition of the head of a family) Thefe, I fay, proclaim the greateft want of that found policy, and good fenfe, which confults the quiet, the happinefs, but above all, the external defence of the individuals committed to its charge. I, my Lord, wifh from my heart, becaufe I think it the advantage of human nature, that no diftinction fubfifted, if poffible, between the nations of the earth; but from a country which is united to ours, I am impatient to fee every diffimilitude removed, which may obftruct our end. Impatient to fee the Scottifh laws approach nearer to the fpirit of our

laws,

laws, and to that fpirit which their anceftors brought from Scandinavia, but afterwards fuffered to evaporate, as I obferved
before. I wifh to fee our jury law, and
whatever laws have any relation to the liberty and property of the fubject, better re-
lifhed by our neighbours; and our common
law, enjoy that preference which it deferves,
to the arbitrary edicts of Roman tyrants:
then fhould we fee minifters of that nation
free from any bias to arbitrary power; and
judges, who fcorning to be tools of defpo-
tifm, in juftice, temper and popularity,
fhould emulate an Holt or a Camden.

As I write without any defign of lower-
ing that brave and prudent people in the
eftimation of their neighbours, and my
ftructure being on the government, and not
the individuals, I hope I fhall ftand acquitted of any view, but that of reducing their
prejudices in favour of any fyftems, which
may prevent that affimilation with England,
for which I have contended. Let Scotland
difcern, acknowledge and imitate, where
England is confefiedly her fuperior; it dero-
gates not from the merit of any fingle perfon of the nation, to make the conceffion,
for it was time, circumftance, fituation,
which have conferred the fuperiority: let
England value not itfelf too much upon this
accidental fuperiority; nor defpife their northern fellow fubjects, for being inferior as a
people,

people, whilſt as individuals, they are in-
conteſtably their equals; and, let them conſider, that the leſſer merit they allow the
Scotch, the more it is the buſineſs of the
Scotch, as a brave and ſpirited nation, to
claim and infiſt upon.

Ireland, my Lord, from the circumſtance
of ſeparation from Great-Britain, ſeems at
firſt view, to want that contiguity, which is,
with juſtice, placed amongſt the eſſentials of
union; but Ireland has every other eſſential,
and though not actually joined to this iſland,
is ſo virtually and in effect; it enjoys very
near the ſame climate, and the genius of its
inhabitants bear as near a reſemblance to
that of the natives of this country, as the
confuſed, undefinable form of 'government
under which they have lived, will admit.
But what ſhould induce us moſt powerfully
of all to beſtow upon it that attention which
union alone can create, is, that Ireland, in
the poſſeſſion of ſome neighbouring powers,
would cauſe a diſadvantage of double its own
intrinſick poſitive value to us; the human
ſpecies has there a moſt ſtrong tendency to
multiplication; the men are brave, hardy
and robuſt; the ſoil fruitful to an uncommon degree; and its harbours commodious,
in every ſenſe of the word. Conceive then,
my Lord, the fatal conſequence of ſo inju-
dicious a treatment of that country, as abſo-
lutely loſe all the benefits which may ariſe

G   from

from it, of flackening the duty and love it is
difpofed to entertain for England. Conceive, my Lord, fuch a country in the poffeffion of an enterprizing French or Spanifh
monarch, who would behold his intereft in
ftrengthening, in cherifhing, and laying it
as a continual check upon Great-Britain; how
much of our regards muft be diverted from
other concerns, by fo refpectable a neigh-
bourhood; when thefe are confidered, with
the great additional ftrength which that
country muft bring to our own, as a part of
one well proportioned body ; the objection
of the want of contiguity immediately va-
nifhes, and we fee Ireland joined to Great-
Britain by a firm political ifthmus.

From the clofeft infpection I have been
able to make into human nature, fuch as it
appears in perufing the hiftory of nations,
or in obferving the actions of cotemporary
individuals (I fpeak of man, modified as he
is by the laws, and education of the particular fociety, of which he is a member, not as
he comes out of the hands of a beneficent
Creator.) It is very difcoverable, that he is
an animal, in whom love * of felf does fo
ftrongly predominate, as to make it very neceffary,

---

* My opinion will not appear morally heterodox, being no more than that man is created with the proper
fize of felf-love, which naturally feeks his prefervation,
but that bad example, bad education, and the artificial
neceffities

ceſſary, that this ungenerous principle be
counteracted by ſome power, which ſhould
have alſo this ſame ſelf-love for its ſource.
Man, were it not for the dread of law,
would think himſelf very excuſable in ſeizing
upon more of the goods of this world, than
by the preſent ſocial methods of acquiring
property, ſhould come to his ſhare ; the fear
of puniſhment conſtantly interpoſes, and
moderation, by degrees, becomes habitual.
In communities, then, man finds a check
upon his deſires in the laws, but, when we
enlarge our view to the whole world, as a
grꝛat aggregate of various communities ; each
community of which, may be compared to
an individual ; where are we to look for the
means of controuling, of bounding, the com-
bined paſſions of the multitudes which form
each community ? How produce moderation?
How curb that ambition in the tyrants of
thoſe communities, which has ſo frequently
deſolated the human ſpecies ? If we, per-
chance, behold national moderation from
peculiar form of government, or what other
cauſe ſoever, prevail in one country, ſo far
from being its ſecurity, that country is
thereby expoſed to the invaſion of ſome per-
fidious neighbour ; the law of nations is re-

---

neceſſities in a ſtate of ſociety, blow it up to an enor-
mous bulk, which would be pernicious, did not the laws
of that ſociety ſuppreſs, what its bad education had given
riſe to.

curred

curred to, but in vain ; a municipal law, the
magiftrate can execute; but to put the law of
nations in force, againft an unruly ftate, the
concurrence of many powers is neceffary ;
this may be prevented by too ftrict a regard
to private intereft, at leaft it may be delayed ;
during that delay towns are deftroyed, provinces feized ; the aggreffing power takes
fuch a hold, as may fupport him through a
ten years war ; at the end of which, want
of union, want of honefty, in fome or all of
thefe powers, who are folemnly confedera-
ted to chaftize him, he has the good fortune
to efcape with impunity the correction :
therefore, which fhould follow a breach of
the law of nations, is not fufficiently certain
to deter the wicked and the ambitious in the
prefent fyftem of Europe. The plan, faid
to have been levied by Henry the Great of
France, was laudable in defign, but impoffible, I think, in execution ; he intended to
bring the joint powers of Europe, who feem
to have interefts the moft oppofite, as near
as poffible to an equality ; that any of thofe
nations who conftituted thefe two general
divifions, may receive protection from their
own party ; when thofe on the other fide,
endeavoured to opprefs them ; but neither he
nor any elfe could afcertain, whofe interefts
were to be the clafhing ones. It was not
thofe of religion, for we fee the Proteftant
religion, every regard to honour, gratitude,
and

and its own real advantage, facrificed by a
once confiderable maritime power, to a narrow, private fcheme of commercial, felfifh
politicks. Auftria and Bourbon were not to
be the contending family interefts, for we
now find them moft clofely, and as we are
pleafed to call it, moft unnaturally connected.
In matters, therefore, fo fluctuaing, it was
impoffible to forefee where, or between
whom the contention fhould be. If Henry
could have enfured one particular ftate,
powerful, and yet honeft enough always to
afford fuccour to the injured, then would he
have fucceeded. Is not the ban of the empire often unjuftly arrayed? And is it not as
often laugh'd at by thofe who are able to op-
pofe it? I fear, my Lord, that human fyftems are not fo capable of perfection, as we,
from our partiality to the framers, are inclined to believe them; but efpecially when
the means of execution are fo complicated,
as in the prefent cafe; and that, therefore,
the moft fimple expedient, for preferving as
general quiet, as the paffions and frailties of
men can poffibly admit, will be, for every
ftate to endeavour at ftrengthening itfelf,
which will make neighbouring powers, for
their own fakes, and the love they entertain for themfelves, beware of violating the
law of nations; fear of each other, will prevent repeated hoftilities, prejudices, which
we obferve to fubfift moft ftrongly between
thofe

thofe who are frequently at war with each other, will languifh and die away, and neighbouring countries, inftead of hating, and feeking · each others mifery, will love and ftudy to promote their mutual happinefs; fo will fear, and an apprehenfion of offending by flow, imperceptible degrees, bring a people firft to bear with its neighbour, then to efteem, and perhaps, in the end, to treat it with cordiality and affection.

I, therefore, muft applaud the wifdom of thofe, who endeavour to multiply virtuous induftrious inhabitants, upon fuch a part of the earth's furface, as may be fufficiently extenfive to form a nation powerful and refpectable, equal to the defence of itfelf againft injury, and able to fuccour a diftreffed neighbour, in cafe of any violence, which may put the common fafety in danger: but fhould equity and moderation be the acknowledged characterifticks of that nation; fhould all the materials for fuch a work be, as it were, already provided by the hand of Providence, and nothing wanting but a proper political combination of them; it is, doubtlefs, under a double obligation of ftrengthening itfelf, becaufe human nature, in general, is deeply interefted in the fafety, in the influence and power of fuch a people; the fmall territory which may be drawn into fuch a community, cannot, with any juftice, complain of being ftripped of their defpicable
ble

ble pretenfions to independency; when, in reality, they are freed from the tyranny of fome proud beggarly duke or count, from the oppreffion of fome paultry republick, and made members of a ftate, where every man's rights are fecured; of a ftate, which is able to maintain real independency; nor can any thing be more evident, than its being for the intereft of all Europe, that no petty fovereignty whatfoever did exift; a temptation to every ambitious neighbour, a caufe of frequent difturbance, and a kind of conftraint upon thofe, who are peaceably difpofed to live in perpetual alarms*.

The provinces of France afford a ftrong example, how diftracted, how miferable that country has been, from the death of Charlemagne until Richlieu's adminiftration, occafioned by the power and influence of the great vaffals of the crown? Was Provence fo happy under her counts; Normandy, Burgundy, Guienne or Britainy, under their Dukes, as they have been fince the monarchy was formed? What fubftantial fatisfaction, could the confideration of being ruled by one of their own country; the vanity and parade of a petty court, whofe retainers devoured the people; afford for the miferies to which the follies and injuftice of their mafters did every

---

* Quia inter impotentes et validos falfo quiefcas. Tacit. de Mor. Ger.

day

day expofe them ? And how can the French, with any juftice, fay they have loft their liberties, becaufe their peers have loft a dangerous power ? And are a people free, becaufe the great lords are able, upon any trifling occafion, to rife up in rebellion againft their king ? I rather believe their flavery more defperate and deplorable. The French, probably, never underftood what real liberty is; for he, who would reftrain the enjoyment of it to any particular order of men, and not fuffer its bleffings to extend through all the virtuous members of the community, miftakes the import of the word. I muft, therefore, approve the political wifdom of the French, for taking in thofe provinces, which feem formed by nature to coincide with their monarchy; the famenefs of language, of manners, of cuftoms, encourageing, and facilitating their defigns; and do think, the accomplifhment was for the general happinefs of thofe provinces, without enquiring what right one nation has to make another happy againft its will. But, when we behold the minifters or tyrants of France, fo iniquitoufly abufing their great increafe of power, by extending their conquefts and influence beyond the limits which nature feemed to prefcribe; and inftead of applying that power to ftrengthen and fecure the quiet of Europe, exerting it on the contrary, in difturbing and deftroying it : we then, indeed,

indeed, muſt lament their greatneſs, and ex-
preſs our ſorrow for that want of rational
liberty, and pure religion, which would, undoubtedly, have produced equity and moderation in the councils of that great monarchy.

The general expediency indeed, neceſſity
of compact, and powerful ſocial aſſociations,
being admitted, the union of Ireland with
Great-Britain appears eaſy and natural, liable to no jealouſies of neighbouring ſtates,
becauſe, the ſovereignty of Great-Britain
over that iſland is univerſally allowed a-
broad ; and that we have always been of
that opinion at home, appears, from having
conſtantly exerciſed it, where the object has
been of ſuch moment, as to affect the intereſt of both kingdoms ; ſuch as ſuperin-
tending their legiſlature, and taking from
their peers a dernier judicial power, left
there ſhould be a failure of juſtice, and de-
population enſue in any part of his Majeſty's
dominions ; and that the leading men of
that iſland are ſenſible of that dependancy is
clear, from their ſubmitting, the very moment it ſeems to anſwer their own private
intereſts, and ſmall ambition, after having
bluſhed, perhaps, for one ſhort ſeſſion, and
ſorely calumniated ſome poor, timid, unpo-
pular ſecretary of their Lord Lieutenant.
Nothing is, therefore, more ſincerely deſired,
than that England ſhould look narrowly into

II   the

the affairs of that country; that it fhould
confider them, in fome refpect, as their own
affairs, and take the proper fteps for bringing the people to a temper for mixing with
themfelves, which having left them fo much
in their own management, has hitherto prevented; nor is it furprizing, that the gentlemen who conftitute the two legiflative branches of that kingdom, fhould be incapable
of moulding their countrymen to the form
we require; their fcheme of government,
and political ideas, are contracted, confined
to raifing fuch fupplies as their governors
fhall demand, eftablifhing turnpikes, and e-
nacting laws againft the growth of Popery;
debates upon the general interefts of Europe,
upon the improvements of commerce, the
prerogative of the crown, or the rights and
liberties of the people, are never heard within their walls — they never afpired to the
bleffings of an habeas corpus act, the ftrongeft proof how fmall their defire of liberty;
carrying with it, at the fame time, the im-
plied confcioufnefs of how little they deferve
it: then, can it be expected from thofe, to
infpire the Irifh with fentiments, which may
entitle them to unite with the freeft, wifeft,
and moft powerful people in Europe? The
landed property of Ireland is, at this time,
vefted in the defcendants of Englifh or Scotch
for the moft part, or held under titles derived from them; the adventurers of Eliza-
beth,

beth, and thofe of the long parliament, being, in truth, the conquerors * of that kingdom, and the purchafers of thofe eftates
which their pofterity now enjoy. The gentlemen of that nation, are therefore fprung
from a warlike anceftry, whofe blood and
t—— were expended in fubduing, and endeavouring to civilize that country which
they now poffefs; and although both from
right and convenience, Ireland is, and ought
to be fubordinate to England, yet, has an
Irifh individual as indifputable a right to liberty and property, as an Englifhman; for
why fhould not the grandfon or great grandfon of an Englifhman, who left his native
country to fight for the glory and advantage
of England, and by his valour and perfeve-
rance eftablifhed a property for himfelf and
family, be looked upon as inferior to the
grandfon or great grandfon of an Englifhman,
who chofe to remain at home? No, my
Lord, the fuperiority is of the aggregate, not
of the individual; it is admitted in one cafe,
becaufe it is for the good of the whole; it is
rejected in the other cafe, becaufe it is quite
unneceffary; and all the gentlemen of Ire-

---

* As for the conquerors of the more early periods;
their defcendants were foon degenerate, fo attached to
the Irifh manners, fo eftranged from thofe of their
Englifh anceftry, that there was a neceffity of conquer-
ing them with the old Irifh, particularly as they were
infected with the fame prejudices againft the reformation.

land

land have the merit of being defcended from a brave and free anceftry. I muft declare, that no people, to whom fo many advantages have been prefented by circumftances moft favourable, did ever fo little avail themfelves of them. England offers to their acceptance, the moft excellent code of laws that was ever framed by any nation; the mildeft and moft rational religion; the foundeft maxims of commerce, and the beft inftructions for the improvement of manufactures: it has afforded them a wholefome example of a ftrict execution of the laws, and moft of thefe proffered kindneffes. It is as certain, that the Irifh reject fuch laws as relate to inheritance, being originally interwoven with our military feudal tenures, which took place upon the firft Englifh fettlement in the ifland, but fubject to the 12th of Charles the Second, are the fame as in England; fo are thofe which relate to perfonal property; the inftitutions which have for their object the manners and principles of the people, independent of religion, are alfo Englifh, but thefe lie dead and unexecuted; thofe which relate to religion, are moftly enacted by themfelves, and are abfurd, unnatural, and fhocking to humanity, I mean the modern Popery laws, which tend to the difcouragement of that fect by forfeiture of property; they are dictated by a fpirit of uncharitablenefs, which never entered

tered into the laws of England, for thefe are remarkable for their lenity and precifion, dictated by a fpirit, which inftead of diffu- fing benevolence amongft the members of a community, deftroys all confidence between man and man, and blafts every bud of ho- nour and virtue ; thefe are executed by bills of difcovery, where breach of faith between neighbours, breach of honour between gen- tlemen, diffolution of the ties of blood be- tween relations, are rewarded with the pro- perty of the perfon againft whom the bill is brought. In England, the nature of a pe- nal law is underftood, and it is a rule that the words of it, are neither to be extended or reftricted by conftruction ; the framers of thefe laws, which have for their object ac- tions not criminal in their own nature, or as the lawyers fay, mala in fe, but only made criminal as they interfere with the policy of the ftate, enumerate the feveral cafes of tranfgreflion, awaken and collect the fubjects attention, point it to the thing which is to be avoided, and leave it not in the power of a judge to fay, that this, or that, was inten- ded by the ftatute, although not particularly expreffed; nor fhall the liberty of any man be taken a way by implication in matters which are morally indifferent. But the Po- pery laws of Ireland are monfters, fome call them penal, others remedial, and all admit, that judges can give them a conftruction,

by

by which their determinations may be at
leaft arbitrary, and the people of that religion left in the greateft confufion and uncer-
tainty. Your Lordfhip fees how great an
enemy to reformation of every kind, how
radically deftructive of all virtue, both publick and private, muft be that body of laws,
which lets loofe, nay, encourages one part of
his Majefty's fubjects to prey upon the other;
how fhould union or brotherly love fubfift,
where legiflature is perpetually founding the
trumpet of difcord? How void of found policy thefe inftitutions, which deftroy the morals of a people under colour of reforming
the religion? That branch of the Popery
laws which are tranfcribed from the Englifh
code, are conceived in a fpirit of fimplicity
and good fenfe; avarice was not the blemifh
of the age which produced them; they do
not ftrip the unfortunate, mifguided, innocent people of their properties, becaufe drawn
into errors by priefts; connived at by magiftrates, whofe duty it is to reftrain their
religious doctrines and difcipline; they may
be executed by juftices of the peace; no
lawyers neceffary, no bills of difcovery, no
profits immediately arifing to any particular
individual, by the execution of thefe laws; it
is religion and the conftitution which are to
receive the advantage, for which reafon they
are feldom put in force; and fince the Popifh
religion is detrimental to the kingdom, the
                                        rigorous

rigorous meafures neceffary for its extirpation fhould be felt, by thofe who caufe the delufion, not by the unfortunate deluded; it is the moutebank, vagabond, impoftor, who fhould be punifhed, and not the fimple, credulous people; fo that inftead of laws which deftroy all confidence, and produce rancour and malevolence between fellow-fubjects, the wicked, felf-interefted propagators, the fly fmuglers of the religion into that unfortunate kingdom, fhould be the object of our indignation. England perfected her reformation by expelling Popifh priefts, fo did the northern ftates, but Ireland expects, by a fcandalous perfecution, to compel a bigotted multitude to reform itfelf, and drive out a fet of men who have now gained a firm eftablifhment in their affections and efteem, and who, I venture to fay, have a greater afcendant over their hearts and confciences, than the moft powerful head of a fept could poffibly enjoy: nor can I fee, how the expulfion of priefts could fail of fuccefs in Ireland; the Romifh fuperftition is fo contrary to common fenfe, to chriftian charity, to the general interefts of the human fpecies, that the clofeft application to the mind, in its circumftances of early, indeed almoft infantine weaknefs, is neceffary to give it root there, the greateft affiduity is required to rear it, but once confirmed, like every other noxious weed, is with great difficulty deftroyed; we,

there-

therefore, perceive thefe dangerous miffiona-
ries, initiating their youth as early as poffible in their fenfelefs myfteries, well know-
ing, that an underftanding, ftrengthened by
reafon, muft ftart at their abfurdities, and reject them with difdain; fo that if the laws
were executed, which would remove thefe
men from the opportunity of practifing upon
the pliant faith of young people; free and
untainted, they would readily embrace a religion founded on reafon and univerfal charity; nor can thefe Romifh ecclefiafticks
complain of perfecution, having felt no effect of the laws enacted againft them, almoft
for an age; they fee and ftudy thofe laws a-
gainft the exercife of Papal jurifdiction, and
yet, fuch is their matchlefs effrontery, as to
hold them at conftant defiance; they are almoft to a man, ill-bred, low-born wretches,
but ever pretending to the gentleman, becaufe defcended from fervants and retainers
in refpectable families, they have impudent-
ly affumed their names; their learning a-
mounts to little more than a bafe unclaffical
fmattering in the Latin tongue, which ena-
bles them to blunder over their maffes, the
rudiments received under an Irifh hedge,
and farther cultivated at fome ftarved French
feminary, in return for which fcanty charity of his Moft Chriftian Majefty, they import into the dominions of his enemy, the
feeds of rebellion, and a total abhorrence
from

from the free fpirit of the Englifh laws and government. What juft caufe of clamour could exift, if his Majefty appointed a fub-fiftence in a foreign country, barely fufficient to keep them from labour during their lives, fubject to this condition, that they never *return to a kingdom where* it is moft certain *they cannot live without* tampering with *con-fciences?* This is a mild expedient for getting rid of a fect, which, for two centuries, has checkt the progrefs of all improvement, and frequently involved that ifland in wars and tumults, by invariably adhering to the fide of fuperftition and tyranny; and I moft heartily wifh to fee this method fubftituted to the punifhment of the innocent, and to the infliction of feverities upon the many, when proper caftigation of a few would better anfwer the purpofe; but I fear the landed intereft of Ireland do not difapprove a policy, which keeps the pofterity of the men whofe forfeited eftates they enjoy, in a ftate of mifery and diftraction, and that, too poignant a remembrance of the cruelties of the Irifh Papifts to their anceftors, inclines them rather to opprefs and enflave the def-cendants of that people, than endeavour fe-rioufly to reform, mix with them in brother-ly love, and be joined as fellow-fubjects by the ties of focial affection.

I well know, that the danger of Popery, has been treated as a bugbear by feveral on

I   this

this fide the water, efpecially by men, whofe
bias to arbitrary principles of government,
prevents their feeing any danger in a fect,
whofe political opinions are the fame with
their own ; they feel not the inconveniencies
that attend it, and are ignorant of the fright-
ful effects of that fuperftition, both here and in
Ireland; their information not exceeding fome
few facts which have happened in their own
time, ftands totally unaided, not only by books,
but even tradition from their parents; they
confider the toafting of memories by the
Irifh Proteftants, as having a tendency to divide the people, and keep ancient animofi-
ties ftill alive ; and it is certain, that a late
high mettled fecretary to a Lord Lieutenant,
had the impudence to pronounce a declama-
tion to that purpofe in the Houfe of Commons of that kingdom, penned, as it is fuppofed, by a remarkable ftile mimick, from
whom that fuborator feems to have received
his impreffions of Irifh affairs, and indeed, of
politicks in general ; had he delivered his
indirect farcafms upon the memory of William the Third, as the opinion of himfelf or
his inftructor; no man who had the leaft
knowledge of either, would have felt any fur-
prize ; but an infinuation of its being the
fenfe of the people of England, that the Irifh
fhould forget the obligations they owe to the
glorious revolution, that they fhould omit any
thing which may preferve it frefh in their
memories,

memories, that they fhould lofe recollec-
tion of what their anceftors fuffered by Popery, from the time of Defmond's rebellion
to the capitulation of Limerick, or lofe fight
of any meafures which humanity will admit, of difabling Popery, from making any
attempts for the future, was, doubtlefs, the
higheft degree of prefumption, that any de-
claimer ever arrived at: England, on the contrary, is well apprized of the undying rancour of that religion, and the almoft irre-
fiftable diffimulation of its chiefs ; how cooly
and fyftematically they proceed in bringing
about their ends, how unrelenting when
poffeffed of any power over their adverfaries;
that the interefts of Proteftanifm are neither
fo clofely, nor uniformly purfued ; that its
profeffors are divided by not acting under
one common head ; not agreeing entirely
either as to doctrine or difcipline ; in fhort,
that they are too indifferent about a religion,
which having reafon on its fide, they look
upon very able to fupport itfelf, and do,
therefore, applaud their Irifh fellow-fubjects
for their caution. It is a ftrong argument
againft fuffering Popery to continue in Ireland, that the progrefs of every good thing
is thereby moft amazingly retarded ; arts and
manufactures are born down by the lazinefs
and want of decent œconomy, which forms
the indelible character of that religion, except in France, where the natural vivacity

of

of the people does, in fome meafure, check
its pernicious tendency; but a much ftronger
it is, that government, that the conftitution
is particularly affected by the evils which
thence enfue, nor can it partake of the free
fpirit of Englifh government, altho' the body
and members are precifely the fame; the
people, like thofe of England, fhare in the
legiflature, by fending reprefentatives to parliament; but to a true conftitutional repre-
fentation, a ftrong relation between the con-
ftituent and the conftituted is abfolutely neceffary, in order to retain the reprefentative
within the bounds of duty, and oblige him
to hold it ever in remembrance, that he is
fent to parliament, not for his own private
advantage, but for that of the publick; the
more confiderable the number of electors,
the more refpectable muft they be in the eyes
of the elected, and the more cautious will
the latter be of neglecting or betraying their
caufe : but whilft the Popifh religion pre-
vails, as to numbers, the body of the people are not reprefented, the individuals of
that perfuafion, lying to a man, under a le-
gal difability of voting at elections; members are fent up to parliament by a few Proteftant freeholders, fo few, as to challenge
very little refpect in the eyes of men, whofe
feats in the houfe have no certain limitation
of time, and thefe fo eafily managed, that
it is very doubtful, whether the fcandalous
neglect

neglect of propagating true religion, which
has appeared in the leading men of that
kingdom, has not proceeded from a notion
that the diffusion of it through the people,
would give them such a weight and authority, as may exact a greater attention from
those who have occasion for their favour,
than has been hitherto found necessary;
and it is not improbable, that a consideration
how much the emoluments of a free trade
in Ireland, must be enjoyed by a body of
men, who are natural enemies to liberty and
the present family, may furnish motives to
England, and for ought I can see, very rea-
sonable ones, for continuing that kingdom
under its present commercial restraints.

Since then, it is evident, that the gentlemen of Ireland, either through a want of
proper training to a more extensive plan of
politicks, or from too close attention to their
present apparent interests, shew a reluctance
in advancing their native country to such a
stage towards perfection, as may bring it to
be of greater use in the general scheme. It
is most incumbent upon England, from a
principle of self-preservation, to observe it
more attentively, as a quarter, by which, in
case of neglect, they are likely to receive a
most deadly blow *.

The

---

* Probably no part of Roman policy was more liable
to cenfure, than their omitting to unite Sicily with Italy,
they

The conftitution of Great Britain has, from caufes very obvicus, taken fince the revolution a dangerous turn to ariftocracy, infomuch, that it is amazing to hear authors of high reputation complain of its tendency to democracy; the Houfe of Commons, it is true, are fuppofed to hold the ftrings of the national purfe : but the majority of that houfe, is certainly formed of men, recommended in counties, but principally in boroughs, by lords ; if they are therefore feptennially created to reprefent the people by the lords, their political opinions and conduct, muft depend upon thofe who create them ; the lower houfe is loft in the upper, and far from being diftinct branches of legiflature, they are virtually, altho' not yet nominally, the fame ; was not this the cafe, all places of truft and profit would not be poffeffed by lords, their relations and dependants : neither as to capacity or induftry, can they claim any fuperiority ; and his Majefty would not be lefs refpectfully ferved, by men who ftood fingly on their perfonal merit and loyalty, than by thofe who are inflated by their own power, or by the confequence and power of thofe who recom-

---

they would have thereby taken from many bad citizens an opportunity of becoming rich, and prevented the dreadful infurrections of their flaves, which lawlefs oppreffion of the wealthy landed intereft of the ifland did occafion.

mend

mend them; but the general bad effects of this evil, being not immediately to my purpose, let us fee how prejudicial it has proved to the interefts of the country I fpeak of. The Lieutenancy of Ireland, is configned of late years, to perfons of the firft rank and title only, and altho' an office upon which depends the advancement of arts, the reformation of religion, and the eftablifhment of government in that kingdom; yet, to the carrying forward of thefe really important works, the fuper-intendancy of a Lord Lieutenant cannot be obtained for more than fix months out of twenty-four; fome, indeed, condefcend to go over a fecond time; fome, out of a confcioufnefs of mifbehaviour, are afraid to venture, and yet their impatience to continue there, does not proceed from any diflike to the profits of the employment, as they prefs moft eagerly at home for every lucrative one, nor from a defire of avoiding the fatigues of a court, for their ambition difclofes itfelf, in the encouragement given to their own little levies at their refpective palaces in Weftminfter, where their dependants pay a conftant attendance; nor from an apprehenfion of lofing the royal favour during abfence, like the unfortunate Effex, but it proceeds from their apprehenfion of lofing their Englifh voters in the houfe, and at elections for members and magiftrates; fo that were it poffible to confine the nobility

to

to the conftitutional range which the law
prefcribes, a double advantage would thence
arife to Ireland ; the prefence of thofe noble
perfonages appointed by his Majefty to be
their guardians and protectors againft domeftick oppreffion, and that the younger
fons of the gentlemen of the kingdom,
would then enjoy a more reafonable proportion of the employments, military, civil and
ecclefiaftick, which their country fo plenti-
fully maintains, than they can in the prefent fituation of affairs, whilft their governors are obliged to beftow them upon their
Englifh dependants, whofe friends and relations have engaged in fupporting their parliamentary influence at home : and here your
Lordfhip fees a great part of the wealth of
one ifland, directed to the ruin of the liberties of the other——But to proceed, if the
chief governor was to continue in the kingdom, he might be at leifure to make progref-
fes, fee whether the people were governed
or oppreffed, and what was the true and general fenfe of the nation; he would there
behold the Proteftant religion expiring thro'
the lazinefs of our priefts, and an unwearied
application in thofe of the enemy; the internal rule of the kingdom or its police, by
which the manners of a people are principally formed, intrufted to magiftrates, whofe
only recommendation is a blind obedience to
the will of thofe, who enjoy the derivative
                                        power

power under the chief governor, and a burn-
ing zeal for extending their interefts at every
election; he would fee the money raifed upon
the people for encouraging manufactures,
and eftablifhing the moft defirable convenience of an inland navigation, perverted to
the vile purpofes of acquiring a dominion
over boroughs, by jobbing the management
of the works to thofe who are able to lend
their affiftance therein ; if he continued his
refidence in the kingdom, he would difcover
laws to have been enacted, which (contrary
to all thofe rules laid down by reafon and
publick utility for the direction of legiflature)
are refpective in their nature, and affume
for their object tranfactions and agreements,
which had an exiftence previous to any notion of making fuch laws, with a view to
encreafe the private fortune of fome parliamentary leaders, or fcreen fome of their fa-
vorite tools from the juft demands of their
fellow-fubjects; he would fee thefe leaders
profefling whigifh revolution principles, and,
indeed, procuring and continuing to themfelves much Proteftant popularity by fuch
appearances, yet, taking every indirect method of fubverting thefe principles, by cor-
rupting univerfally, and erafing from the
minds of their countrymen, every impreffion
of honour and regard to liberty ; he would
fee the common people labouring under all
the miferies of poverty, of flavery, and daily

K   finking

finking from bad to worfe; and he would lay the true ftate of that unfortune kingdom before his Majefty, from whofe wifdom and goodnefs it could not fail of redrefs.

But if an unbounded attention to their parliamentary concerns, has fo entirely engroffed the body of the Britifh nobility, as to render it impoffible to find thofe amongft them, who will dedicate their time to a real difcharge of their duty as a Lord Lieutenant of Ireland; many commoners may be found, who with great juftice, will think themfelves highly honoured by the office, even under that *fevere condition* of doing their duty: the office derives no luftre from the perfon, but the perfon from the office; a rule, which will hold even with kings. It is allowed, that to the exercife of an office in the treafury, admiralty, or the other departments of government, fome experience and application are required, but for the government of a kingdom, which contains above two millions of inhabitants, fupports, as I am informed, twenty thoufand men, with placemen and penfioners beyond number, a nobleman becomes inftantaneoufly qualified; and when he thinks proper to be weary of his charge, his fucceffor becomes as fuddenly, and as miraculoufly qualified as he. If a country is fo far removed from the refidence of the fovereign, that he cannot fee with his own eyes the real ftate of that country; and

if

if the indolence or avocation of viceroys are
fuch, that they will not fee with their own
eyes, but muft receive the *reprefentations*,
which they lay before Majefty, from men
whofe private intereft it is, that every thing
fhould be *mifreprefented*; then will a few families of large fortunes, and extenfive con-
nexions, play off the king againft the people, and the people againft the king, and
with the greateft fuccefs, provided they are
ftrengthened by an Englifh intereft, they
will appear to the people poffeffed of the
royal confidence, from the power they are
feen to have of beftowing fome trifling civil
employments, at times, a commiffion in the
army, and upon extraordinary occafions, perhaps, a bifhoprick; and the loyal deportment of the people will, by a moft fcandalous impofition, be imputed not to its real
caufe, a thorough *fenfe of their duty*, *and an
unalterable affection to their Prince*, but to the
addrefs and ingenious management of thefe
leaders; this, I may venture to undertake,
is the hinge upon which Irifh government
has long turned, and the confequence muft
be an abfolute vaffalage in that country, and
an entire obftruction of all intercourfe between King and people; the feelings of al-
legiance will become faint; dependance,
fear, adoration of their domeftick idols, will
take place, and thefe idols will have it in
their power at length, to extort from their

mafter

maſter whatever ſpecies of penſion, or gratification, they, in the plenitude of their inſolence, ſhall think proper to demand.

However, ſince the age in which we live is ſuch, that an unſocial, contracted ſelfiſhneſs, appears the ſtrongeſt line in its character, I ſhould not, my Lord, be ſurprized to hear it urged, in oppoſition to my ſpeculations; *If Ireland is of ſo great moment, ſo fruitful in ſoil, its inhabitants ſo numerous, with ſuch variety of other advantages,* why ſhall it not take care of itſelf? to this it may be ſufficient to reply, that from her political dependance upon England, ſhe cannot venture to undertake any buſineſs of weight, or of conſiderable import to herſelf, without the conſent of England, bold *ſtrokes of reformation come from the arm which is powerful and unconſtrained;* that Ireland, backward as ſhe is in copying from England, whatever may be uſeful and praiſe-worthy, has been moſt ſingularly docile in the ſcience of cabal and domeſtick intrigue, nor are her ſons leſs expert in bribery and corruption, than the managers of the moſt diſputed borough in England: we have, therefore, rendered them both unfit and undiſpoſed to reform themſelves, whilſt their ſubordination, had they been never ſo well diſpoſed, has put it entirely out of their power; but if this reply proves inſufficient, arguments drawn from love of ſelf, muſt have their due weight,

weight; and let us recollect, that a time may come, when some powerful state, less indifferent about the advantages which nature offers, may think seriously of that country, which we look upon as unmeriting our notice; that the misconduct of governors, or the under agents of governors, may create an indifference in the minds of the people, whether they live under an Irish Lord Lieutenant, a French commandant, or a Spanish viceroy; that the united disaffections of the inhabitants, both Protestant and Papist, must yield great encouragement to foreign attempts to invade them, and almost certain stability to their invasions; and that in some future luxurious, degenerate age, a Hawke or Kepple may not appear, whose matchless intrepidity shall brave the dangers of rocks and shoals, to destroy the destined invaders, perhaps, the conquerors.

OUR PLANTATIONS have formed the subject of so much debate and altercation of late, that little new, and therefore very little interesting, can be now advanced upon that head; yet how will this matter appear, upon trial by that real touchstone of all political disquisitions, *improvement of manners and publick security?* Moral perfection, or the nearest possible approaches thereunto, is indisputably the first, and most worthy end of all our pursuits; and yet defence against external violence, protection of the community

engages,

engages, and with reason, almost an equal
share of our attention, being that, without
which, an opportunity of affecting the former is absolutely lost; arts, sciences, and
pure religion, no more than eloquence *,
can have their natural growth, amidst the
strugglings for liberty, amidst the shouts of
conquest, or, indeed, amidst the fears and
apprehensions of being conquered; to this
purpose is required a steady, settled, unpalli-
able temper in the state, for which reason,
many small considerations must give way to
this single great one; agreeable, therefore,
to this principle, I cannot avoid declaring,
that our American fellow-subjects have not
maturely considered how trifling are the re-
strictions of the mother country, when
weighed against the advantages, which that
same mother country has afforded them; and
I consider every writer who would whet the
edge of their appetites, to a higher degree of
keenness, for trade and wealth, as the general
enemy, who would raise them too high in
their own opinions, and lessen, in their eyes,
the obligations they must owe to England:
they talk of having carried *their fortunes
from England to make their settlements*; some
particular men might have done so, but,

---

* Neque enim in constituentibus rempublicam, nec
in bella gerentibus, nec regum dominatione devinctis,
nasci cupiditas dicendi potest. Cicero de Oratore.

nothing is more certain, or better known, than that neceffity has been the caufe of al- moft every emigration that has happened, and that the beginnings of moft American properties were remarkably flender : by a free and beneficial trade, well protected by Britifh navies, they have, indeed, accom- plifhed a moft rapid growth, to which their own much to be applauded care and induf- try has largely contributed.——The rifque, *they fay, they have run in making their fettlements* cannot, as they pretend, be admitted as done with a view of *ferving the mother country*, be- caufe, in general, countries are allowed to fuffer rather, by the exportation of their wealth and inhabitants, and fo would Eng- land, did not the peculiarity of its naval and commercial circumftances, fo fingularly dif- tinguifh it from Spain and all other coun- tries ; did not its dominion of the feas, fo fa- cilitate the intercourfe between every branch of its empire, that any of its inhabitants, or the property of any of its inhabitants, may, as it were by magick, virtually and in effect, appear wherever they require. Now, as to their obligations to Britain, admitting that no pecuniary aids had been advanced to- wards eftablifhing their fettlements, how can they difcharge themfelves of the obligation of having received from England a body of excellent laws, ready to be tranfcribed ; a fet of focial improved manners, ready to be

tranf-

tranfplanted ; arts and fciences ; all which, if raifed from the feed, would have a tedious, and interrupted growth in the wilds of A-merica ? If we add to this, that refpect which a fubject of England muft challenge, in what fituation foever, which no fmall colony could pretend to maintain, it will be impoffible to liften with patience, to the man, who would refine away thefe obliga-tions, by alledging that England has acted from narrow motives, in order to ftrengthen herfelf : an undutiful child, may tell his fa-ther, that he begot him to pleafe himfelf ; that he cherifhed him, that he fixed him and his fortunes in the world, merely to gratify his parental feelings ; and upon this falfe reafoning, impioufly hold himfelf acquitted of every duty ; but nature declares againft him ; and altho' no ingratitude can dwell where there is a reciprocation of good offices, yet, he who receives the firft act of kind-nefs, will ever remain the moft obliged.

No man entertains a more cordial affec-tion for our fellow-fubjects of America than I do ; their emotions in favour of liberty are generous and praife-worthy, but muft ftill be of opinion, that they have not, as yet, con-ceived (fo generally as may be wifhed) no-tions of government fufficiently digefted and extenfive ; fince their anceftors made their emigrations, liberty has received many and great improvements ; the rude wild ftock,

hurried

hurried by fcandalous perfecutions at home, they haftily plucked from the mother foil; it ftruck ftrong roots, and vigoroufly flourifhed in their new congenial clime; but it was at the revolution, the generous well-flavoured fruit was engrafted, which I fear, no part of the Britifh empire, except England, has yet brought themfelves properly to relifh.

A facred and inviolable right of taxing themfelves, and regulating their own affairs, without any exception, for what unforefeen dangers and fudden emergencies may produce, has been contended for with too great a latitude; the colonies muft now confider themfelves as a part infeparable from the grand body of the Britifh empire, and as fuch, an evil happening to that part, may fpread itfelf to the whole, as a fore in any particular member, may caufe a general mortification; inattention to, or bad management of the plantations, may let in an evil, which would, in its confequences, bring the exiftence of Great-Britain into danger; a moment's deliberation, then, muft furely fix the relative weight of Britifh trade, glory, and influence, to that of American pure natural liberty, and abfolute, uncontroulable independance. The Americans, being the fubject of the prefent debates, becaufe they happen to be more immediately concerned, declare themfelves the proper judges upon

the

the occafion, but altho' moft *immediately* concerned, they do not furnifh the objeƈ of *greateſt* concern; Britifh fafety, power and trade, furnifh this grand objeƈ : Britain, therefore, is the more competent judge, and it would be unreafonable to expeƈ, that any wife adminiftration, after the warnings already received from the indolent deportment of the colonies at the beginning of the late war, would fuffer confiderations of fo high a nature, to reft upon the determinations of men, whofe negleƈ has been already fo juftly cenfured, from whofe torpid fullennefs and obftinacy, the enemy did confeffedly derive fuch advantage. Shall it depend upon the refolutions of a Philadelphian affembly, whether our fellow-fubjeƈs fhall arm in defence of liberty and property? Does the fate of a whole continent bear any proportion to an almoft imperceptible encroachment upon the important privilege of an American, deliberating for a year or two, whether he will pay fix-pence in the pound, to fave himfelf and family from perdition? A provincial affembly is very capable of determining upon what is moft expedient for their own internal rule, what moft advantageous to their trade; but when the great fcheme of governing all the parts of an extenfive community, when the relation in which they ftand to this community is to be confidered, then their capacities begin to

narrow

narrow in my eftimation, and they come to fhew themfelves in a fphere of debate, for which I can, by no means, think them qualified. Why, fays an individual, fired with a wild fpirit of liberty, fhall I give up that power which nature has beftowed upon me, of acting and thinking for myfelf? Why, fays an advocate for fociety, fhall you be protected by fociety in your property and perfon, in the exercife of virtuous liberty, which is a power of doing, not what you will, but what you ought to will? If no individual then, may fet up his fingle opinion and ftrong cravings for crude liberty, where focial good is concerned, if he is not allowed to difcern fo clearly, whether thefe loud calls of nature, about which he makes fo great a parade, may not interfere with, and obftruct fome moral and focial end; no more is any diftinct part of an empire, intitled to carve for itfelf, and lay it down as an invariable maxim, that on no occafion whatfoever are they to be governed, by rules to which they have not confented; much refpect, therefore, is due to the opinion of Great-Britain, in that material point of regulating a provincial defence, and whenever it fhall be urged, that the Americans are moft competent to judge of the quantity of taxation, or the method of applying the taxes, and that a want of provincial defence, muft be more immediately and fenfibly felt by

L 2 them-

themſelves, than by thoſe who are far removed from the ſcene of American affairs ;
when they plead the great law of nature and
of liberty, to any claim of Britain to ſuper-
intend their affairs, I reply, the ideas of ſocial liberty in diametrical oppoſition to their
allegations, I aver, that they are not the
moſt competent judges of the expediency of
a domeſtick defence; and I eſtabliſh my
averment, by their having already ſhewn
themſelves incompetent, in never producing
any one general plan for that purpoſe, from
the peace of Utrecht to the war of 1756;
infomuch, that altho' ten times the number
of our enemy, they would have been abſo-
lutely driven off the continent, were it not
for the ſeaſonable interpoſition of England,
and all this, from a peeviſh reluctance to af-
ſociate and unite, a reluctance, to ſacrifice a
ſmall part of their own will and pleaſure, to
peace and ſecurity, which reluctance, they
are diſpoſed to compliment, with the honourable appellation of liberty.

If then, the American colonies, have ma-
nifeſted a neglect to make the neceſſary pro-
viſion for their own defence, and that Britain
may ſuffer through this neglect, ſhe is powerfully warranted in proceeding againſt a pro-
bability of any future ſituation of thoſe colonies, ſo dangerous, ſo productive of heavy
expence, as that we have lately beheld. It
was, indeed, the duty of the colonies, to an-
ticipate

ticipate the cares of the mother country, and make, after the example of Ireland, fuch a military eftablifhment as may tend to difcourage any attempts of an enemy, and not furnifh, by their remifnefs, a Britifh adminiftration, with even an excufe for obtruding their kind offices upon them : they fhould confider the various and fluctuating nature of Britifh councils; and that power, from the free nature of our government, may be fometimes in the hands of men, who are delighted in obliging and ftrengthening our enemies, in ill-treating and difgufting our friends, and who, when they accidentally engage in carrying even a neceffary meafure into execution, ftumble upon fome mode of doing it, which not only deftroys every end and advantage which may arife from it, but is alfo productive of univerfal murmurs and diffatisfaction; but of all things, fhould they beware of beholding our minifterial blunders, in the light of national acts, and thence, perhaps, conceive a diflike or alienation of affection from their Britifh fellow-fubjects. The fenfe of this nation is neither unjuft, unreafonable, or oppreffive; but no human wifdom will, I fear, be ever able to fecure us againft falling fometimes into the hands of fuch wretches, as thofe who made the peace of Utrecht or of Verfailles.

On the other fide, my Lord, it muft be admitted, that the mother country has not en-

entirely acquitted herfelf in the difcharge of
her parental offices. It is certainly the duty
of thofe, whom Providence has commiffion-
ed by conferring great powers on them, for
promoting the welfare of the human fpecies,
to watch and attend to the changes of circumftance, which muft happen to all earthly
things, and frame fuch inftitutions, as may
anfwer (fo far as human prudence can pro-
vide) to the variety of cafes which may arife;
new circumftances produce new fyftems.
When a perfonal property began to grow
confiderable in England, our anceftors
thought proper immediately to enact fuch
laws, as might facilitate alienations; they had
recourfe to the civil codes, and thence they
brought the ftatute of will of diftributions,
and adopted fuch a portion of the fpirit of
Roman jurifprudence, as may anfwer the
exigency. But, with regard to colonies, fo
diftinguifhed is Great Britain, fo critically
diftinguifhed, by a complication, of naval,
of landed, of commercial, of military confiderations, from every ancient ftate; that inftitutions drawn from Tyre, from Carthage,
from Rome, or from Rhodes, can never anfwer the prefent occafion; and legiflature
muft inveftigate, thro' the walks of nature,
morals of utility, and of prefent convenience,
fuch truths as may afford a ground work for
this neceffary undertaking; our common
law, revered with juftice for its honeft fimplicity,

plicity affords no refources in fo variegated
a fubject; nor could our Gothick fore-fathers
poffibly forefee the aftonifhing turn, which
this kingdom has taken to commercial ad-
venture, fince the reign of Henry the Seventh,
occafioned by a moft unexpected event, the
difcovery of a new world; they could not
forefee the emigration of colonies to this
new world, and could, therefore, never
think of framing any calculation for fuch a
contingency : why, then, look into the laws
in being, for any aids upon this occafion?
A plaufible and fagacious lawyer, may difcover fomething in his books analogous, or
what he thinks, and would perfuade the
world is analogous to the cafe of our colonies, propofed to him for ferious confideration; he fancies it a corporation, for inftance,
and from henceforth, every American quef-
tion, comes to be examined by principles
laid down for directing a corporate legiflature; that is, becaufe a Britifh corporation
has delegated their natural original right of
legiflature, to thofe who reprefent them in
parliament, and thereby vefted in that affembly, a power of controuling their corporate acts : our colonies, therefore, who not
being called upon, make no returns of members to the Britifh parliament, are fubject to
a like controul, this is not reafon, either
plain or refined, either natural or artificial,
and therefore cannot be law; in truth, the
opinions

opinions of the gentlemen of the long robe, are not to be admitted, in an affair, so much above their level, for this would, indeed, be an erecting of courts, intended for explication of the laws in being, into actual legislatures; a power, very lately rejected by, perhaps, one * of the wisest and most modest judges, that ever adorned a bench ; and, in a case, where the exercise of such a power would be readily excused, being in vindication of the liberty of the subject. But, my Lord, the laborious strainings of our lawyers, in applying their learning to American affairs, will never produce any thing adequate to this grand occasion ; our colonies are insensibly grown into a respectable importance, and demand the most solemn consideration of legislature, of wise, of honest legislature; and, I am persuaded, that the present matter deserves treaties, commissioners, and every other solemnity, preceding the act which u-united these kingdoms ; we should conciliate the good-will of our fellow-subjects, who live at a distance, as warmly as that of those who are nearer home, provoke neither to resentments, by injury or oppression, but ever remember, that Egina and Æubea were easily brought to a sense of duty, by the Athenians, whenever they became turbulent ; but

---

* Judgment delivered by Lord Camden, in the case of Entick and the Messengers, last day of Michaelmas term, 1765.

when

when they carried their arms againſt Greeks,
who were more diſtant, the ruin of their
power was the immediate conſequence, and
their greatneſs expired at Syracuſe *.

Had Britain been bleſſed with a continu-
ance of that adminiſtration, which carried
her military glory to ſo exalted an height, in
the laſt war, had that miniſtry, I ſay, been
permitted to conclude a ſound and healthy
peace ; upon that firm baſis, by ſuch able
political builders, would have been raiſed a
pile, compoſed of all our colonies and de-
pendencies, whoſe ſtrength, beauty, and
magnificence, would be the envy and admi-
ration of the world ; theſe wiſe and virtuous
patriots, would have ſhewn talents for peace,
equal to thoſe they had diſplayed for war,
and our conqueſts, inſtead of being the cauſe
of diſſentions and animoſities, between his
Majeſty's loyal ſubjects, would long ſince
have turned to great and laſting account :
commiſſioners would be formally appointed
to examine minutely into the ſtate of our
colonies ; a proper method taken for raiſing
ſupplies to anſwer the expences of government ; taxations be laid, in a manner, the
leaſt grievous to the ſubject, and moſt con-
ſiſtent with ſocial liberty ; in ſhort, that
gradual aſſimilation with the mother country, ſo much to be deſired by all its deſcen-
dants, would be at length brought about ;

---

* The Syracuſans were a Dorick colony.

M · for

for though war is the feafon of danger, yet,
is it very eafily demonftrated, that the minifter of peace is as much above the minifter of
war, as the ends are more worthy than the
means; that is, when the great and neceffary
works of peace are properly attended to ; but
when peace is made, in order to generate
matter for new war; then, indeed, the artful wretch, who can deceive his king, corrupt, debafe, and opprefs the people, will
anfwer every purpofe ; no neceffity for integrity or wifdom remains, where cunning and
deceit are found to be all-fufficient.

I am,

My LORD, *&c.*

F I N I S.

www.ingramcontent.com/pod-product-compliance
Lightning Source LLC
Chambersburg PA
CBHW031448270326
41930CB00007B/911